The Spirit of Cheltenham

The Spirit of Cheltenham

KENSINGTON WEST

PRODUCTIONS

Kensington West Productions Ltd
5 Cattle Market, Hexham, Northumberland NE46 1NJ
Tel: (01434) 609933, Fax: (01434) 600066

Photography by
Thoroughbred Photography Ltd; principally Trevor Jones
with Gill Jones and Laura Green with contributions by Ed Byrne
and Caroline Norris. Additional photography by
Racecourse Photographer Max Le Grand.
www.thoroughbredphoto.com
01638 713944

Editors
Julian West & Barry Roxburgh

Designed by
Nick Ridley

Origination by
Pre-Press Ltd, Hong Kong

Printed in China

Frontispiece: Turning for the long downhill run for home at the foot of Cleeve Hill. **TJ**

Title Page: Owner John Hales and connections help jockey Ruby Walsh celebrate Azertyuiop's memorable Arkle win. **TJ**

Facing Title Page: Sunrise over Lambourn, home of many a Cheltenham champion. **TJ**

Facing: Irish jockey Barry Geraghty. **TJ**

Left: Up the hill to home in the Fulke Walwyn Kim Muir chase. **TJ**

Contents

Articles

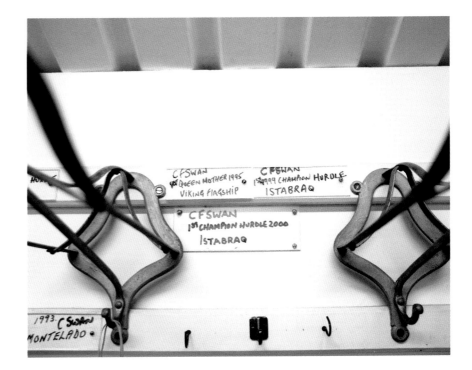

Top: Thierry Doumen urges home Baracouda to take the Bonusprint Stayers' Hurdle, 2003. *TJ*

Bottom: Charlie Swan's pen records Istabraq's three consecutive Smurfit Champion Hurdle victories in the weighing room. *TJ*

Facing: Cheltenham Managing Director Edward Gillespie. *TJ*

Introduction by Edward Gillespie, Managing Director, Cheltenham Racecourse

You could spend hours trying to list all the different ingredients that make the experience of watching the races at Cheltenham so special. To start there's the backdrop and the winter sun gleaming off Cleeve Hill. Then you have the swing of the course that one moment takes the runners past grazing cattle without a soul in sight and the next, it swallows them up in a cauldron of sound as the strip of green thrusts through the very heart of the crowd. Glance around and you are reminded of past triumphs. The stands may have changed out of all recognition but the same turf carries the Champions of today that bore Golden Miller, Cottage Rake and Arkle. Generations of spectators come and go but the faces do not alter.

'Cheltenham' means far more than just a stylish Regency town that fills to the brim each March. The very name stands for the anticipation from the moment the last betting slip falls to the ground one year to that sensation as another is held firmly in the hand and the contenders for the Gerrard Supreme Novices move up to the starting line. It stands for the roar as the favourite stalks the struggling pacemakers at the top of the hill. It translates into the sensation of cheering in the winner that touched off your banker and the smiling at complete strangers who appear to have tears in their eyes.

The Spirit of Cheltenham will strike when you least expect it. Turn the page of a gnarled racecard on a glorious summer's evening hundreds of miles from the Cotswolds and the sky will suddenly be leaden and charged with emotion. Stroll into a country pub high on the Fells and faded photographs from old calendars whisk you back to the sixties with Mill House in his pomp and some tale from across the water that must be an exaggeration. Visit the course itself; walk up to those fences and you could be treading on a giant in his slumbers. Catch the sound of horses galloping in the distance and, in a moment, you are there with 50,000, straining to hear the name of your fancy.

Cheltenham is also a time. A week in March, a weekend in November, cold Saturdays in December and January, a party at New Year and back slapping incredulity on an April evening. 16 days for an entire season. Blink and you've missed it for another year.

Tens of thousands have been to Cheltenham without ever stepping foot in Gloucestershire. Gathering at preview evenings to hear each race dissected or gazing through shop windows at silent images; each one is touched by the concentration of effort, the wafer thin margin betwixt winning and defeat, months of preparation, frustration and exhilaration. The next best thing to being at Cheltenham is thinking about being there. And coming back.

Cheltenham is a dream.

Above: Nicky Henderson's first lot. *TJ*

Facing: Istabraq and Charlie Swan (left) lead PJ Colville and Darapour over Aidan O'Brien's Ballydoyle schooling hurdles. *CN*

Chapter One

Living with a Dream

Left: Seeing eye to eye: Henrietta Knight shares a thought with her Best Mate. **TJ**

Facing: Michael Hourigan and Doran's Pride (centre) out hunting with the Strawhall Harriers. A fatal fall at Cheltenham ended the Irish horse's distinguished career at 14 - winner of the '95 Bonusprint Stayers' Hurdle and third in two Tote Gold Cups. **CN**

Even the best laid plans can go awry when mother nature turns her joker card as snow halts the 1987 Tote Gold Cup. *TJ*

Double trouble: Riders and horses hit the deck going full tilt. *EB*

Above: They're off and running!
After the start in the Royal &
SunAlliance Novices Hurdle. *TJ*

Below: Jaques Ricou and Jair du
Cochet, second in the Royal &
SunAlliance Chase. *TJ*

Facing: Tightly packed birch. *TJ*

Above: Hats off to the winner: Rooster Booster's owners Mr and Mrs Terry Warner share the glory of a Smurfit Champion Hurdle win. *TJ*

Facing: Michael Bowe leads top stayer Limestone Lad home after exercise. *CN*

Chapter Two

Preparation

Getting Prepared *by Alan Lee*

For the true devotees, and there are a lot of us around The Festival preparations have no beginning and no end. They are a constant, the intensity and piquancy merely varying according to the time of year. I know of a lot of folk - and call them sad at your peril - who annually celebrate the day in September when the next Festival is closer than the last. Even allowing for bias, I can think of no other sporting or cultural event that generates such dedicated ardour.

The Cheltenham timetable is no different for the trainers, though the anticipation may be tinged with apprehension and darkened by responsibility. How often have you heard a novice hurdle winner in October touted as "a likely Festival type"? And, if such lofty ideas are being made public in October, it can be depended upon that the connections of the animal - even those hardened by experience - have harboured them for at least the previous six months.

I once asked Nicky Henderson, the estimable Lambourn trainer who is now very much a respected senior of his profession, when he began preparing for The Festival. "As soon as the last one is finished," came the answer. And he was not joking. It has to be this way, in the best-run stable yards, for the importance of Cheltenham, within the natural rhythms of a National Hunt season, is impossible to overrate. Some say it is too dominant. What nonsense. The truth is that it gives the sport a focus, an annual finals day, envied by so many.

It is not just the prize money, though that is a significant lure, nor even the prestige associated with having horses run well at Cheltenham. It is the whole, consuming atmosphere of The Festival that acts as the perennial magnet. If you seek an involvement in jump racing, then you crave even a small part of the March jamboree that dominates it. To spend Cheltenham week in a vacuum, with no credible runners, is a failure that many yards find hard to bear.

Though the importance of Cheltenham as a sacred week of the year is now engraved on my brain, I came to it late, and by a circuitous route that took in a number of other sports. Introduced to jumping by some cricketing friends, a first trip to Cheltenham was not long delayed. I was first intrigued by the lifestyle and endeavours of the human combatants - the jockeys and trainers - rather than the horses themselves. Familiarity finally bred a rounder interest, though for me the people-watching at The Festival will always be as important and rewarding as the horse-watching. To observe the trainers in the minutes leading up to one of the many championship races at this peerless meeting is to acquire a stake in a swirl of human emotions. This day, this hour, these few minutes is what the entire season has been about and, in their different ways, every one of the trainers on view will betray the enormity of the moment. Martin Pipe might be making copious notes in his racecard as he studies the opposition but, beneath the professional instinct, even the long-time champion will be feeling the strain. Lesser mortals will show it by talking too much or too little, or by needing a stiff drink before the appearance in the great amphitheatre that is the Cheltenham paddock.

The elusive key, of course, is to bring horses to their peak for mid March. It sounds simple enough - everyone knows when The Festival is, each year, and it is surely only like planning the training of any human athlete? Except that it is not. What these trainers are contending with, each year, are the imponderables of their profession - the weather patterns of a British winter which affect training regimes and ground conditions on course; the health of their horses, that may deteriorate without warning or explanation; and the propensity of many jumps horses to put in an unaccountably poor run, or suffer a fall, just when it is most vital that they maintain equilibrium.

It is when these setbacks occur that the fibre of a yard is tested. Cheltenham may be only weeks away and the best-laid plans have been aborted. The trainer and staff will be under a unique brand of pressure now, for there is no consolation, nor even any truth, in the platitude that there will be another day. There is only one Cheltenham each year and no-one wants to miss it.

Visiting stable yards in the weeks before The Festival is a tradition, eagerly pursued by journalists such as myself and nervously tolerated by the majority of trainers. Even those who are cordially communicative for 11 months of the year tend to become brusque, short-tempered and impatient with those who ask foolish questions or take a step that might startle a temperamental horse. And can you blame them?

Last year, as Cheltenham approached, the focus of attention fell squarely on the Oxfordshire hamlet of West Lockinge and the charming, farmyard base of Henrietta Knight. It was here that Best Mate, the brightest chasing star to emerge in two decades, was being prepared to win his second Tote Gold Cup. Night and day, the trainer and her bucolic husband, Terry Biddlecombe, were assailed by requests and queries, not only from the media but also the public. They handled it all with patience and goodwill but when Tote Cheltenham Gold Cup day arrived, both looked exhausted by the effort.

It was only later that they revealed the truth, that Best Mate's preparations had gone badly awry in the previous autumn and that they had lived with the dread of another setback. At times like this, there is no wider perspective in the lives of those who prepare horses for Cheltenham. The Festival, and its implications, takes them over totally.

So this year, when your countdown is complete and the great day dawns, when you drive over Cleeve Hill and feel that churning in the pit of the stomach as the Gerrard Supreme Novices Hurdle and all that follows beckons you down to Prestbury Park, spare a thought for those whose anticipation is coloured by so many unspoken fears.

Above: Beef or Salmon and Michael Hourigan. *CN*

Facing: Trainer Edward O'Grady on his hunter Tatter with dog Eric as the string returns home on the all weather gallop. *CN*

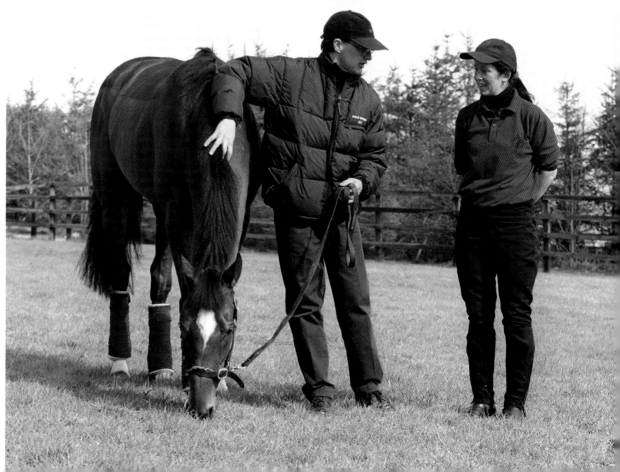

Left: Pride and joy: Willie Mullins and Florida Pearl. *CN*

Below: Lean on me: Aidan O'Brien takes time out with Istabraq and groom Anita Harvey. *CN*

Race you home: Darapour leads Istabraq (left) with Pat Lillis up, while Kilcash Castle and Theatreworld follow on as Aidan O'Brien supervises from the jeep. *CN*

Left: Round the bend: Willie Mullins watches Florida Pearl (left) and Alexander Banquet cantering on. **CN**

Above: Irish pride: Danoli with Padraic English up and trainer Tom Foley on the hill above the village of Myshall. **CN**

Above, left and facing: All in a morning's work for a busy trainer.

From his base at Seven Barrows in Lambourn Nicky Henderson has sent out 25 Festival winners including two Bonusprint Stayers' Hurdles and three Smurfit Champion Hurdles with old favourites such as Remittance Man and See You Then. **TJ**

After a quick prod to test the going, Nicky Henderson puts stable stars Dusk Duel and Geos through their paces at Seven Barrows. **TJ**

Returning on the all weather gallop at West Lockinge. *TJ*

Henrietta Knight has sent out five Festival winners courtesy of stable stars such as Best Mate and Edredon Bleu from her base at West Lockinge Farm near Wantage, Oxfordshire. *TJ*

Hard at work... the life of a stable never stops   *TJ*

Facing: Whether they win or lose Paul Nicholls' horses are treated like stars.

Nicholls supervises second lot at Manor Farm in Somerset. From here he has
captured some notable Festival trophies including See More Business' 1999 Tote
Gold Cup and Arkle victories for Flagship Uberalles and Azertyuiop. *TJ*

Martin Pipe's Pond House
field and Pond House
stableyard. *TJ*

Hen and Terry back at the ranch. *TJ*

Trainer Venetia Williams makes sure her charges are out in the field as much as possible. Here with an old favourite, the grey Teeton Mill (above) winner of a Pertemps King George VI Chase and Hennessy Gold Cup. Her Festival successes also include wins by the plucky mare Lady Rebecca and Samakaam in the Grand Annual. *TJ*

The dream lives on. *CN*

Facing: Breakfast for early risers. *EB*

Chapter Three

Getting Organised

Don't fence me in. David's Lad ponders an insurmountable obstacle. *EB*

Early morning racecourse gallops attract a crowd of connections and the curious.   *EB*

Top: Arriving in style: no queues in cars for The Queen as she arrives at the racecourse. *TJ*

Left: More media for the scrum with John Inverdale. *MLG*

Left: Think Thomas the Tank Engine and we'd go odds on you'd guess his name. *TJ*

Top: 'Tis surely only fitting that the Irish sponsor this race. *TJ*

Never mind the spin: BBC Radio 5 Live's Cornelius Lysaght chats with Jockey Club PR Director John Maxse (right). *TJ*

The Roar *by Richard Edmondson*

There is a sound at The Festival that is the sweetest in all sport. It is the guttural, glorious roar, the rumble from the stands when the runners depart on their way to the first obstacle in the Gerrard Supreme Novices' Hurdle. It is the breaking of the spell of anticipation.

It is The Festival's destiny that the meeting falls at the end of the longest of drum rolls, one enough to turn the sticks to sawdust. Barely has one gathering in Gloucesetrshire dispersed before the expectation for the next takes seed. The waiting ends only with the roar.

It is a strange apprehension that floods in when you first enter the Prestbury Park precincts in mid-March, a hope that you have not cheated yourself, slackened the leash too much on the emotions. Yet The Festival never disappoints. The roar always gets you.

"That great noise is not for the horses," Edward Gillespie, Cheltenham's managing director, says. "It's by the people for the people, a sense of kinship, that we have all, the English and Irish in particular, made it together again for this greatest of communal events."

Cheltenham is a great sensory jungle and at times an uncomfortable one. Racegoers may complain about the mash once they leave Cheltenham but they never do so while they are there. The answer is too easy. And they come back to this crunch in the Cotswolds, look forward to it.

It gets them all does The Festival, even the most successful, the most inured to flights of fancy. Martin Pipe, who has won more races at the games than any trainer, believes he sees a different man on Festival morn.

"It only really hits me when I'm having that last-minute shave before I set off for the races," he says. "Just at that point I think to myself "what on earth am I doing? Suppose I get no winners". Everyone seems to think I've got six certainties, which makes me really nervous. I begin to panic.

"Luckily, I'm quite busy while all the anxiety and the excitement is building up. But, just before the first race, I'm in the stands there and the heart really starts to beat. I can almost hear it getting louder and louder. Then it's that huge, fantastic roar from the crowd and you can finally settle down with the bins. You're off."

There is salivation between each race, but nothing to compare with the initial build-up. Many racegoers have used careful husbandry to put together a war chest, but what has been compiled over 12 months is ready to be jeopardised over half that number of races.

There are small men with big money, and big men with the largest wagers that will be staked all year. For while the racecourse itself can be a dangerous place for horses - the best horses travelling at the fastest pace - there is peril too on the other side of the running rails. Bookmakers do not at least lose their lives at Cheltenham, but there remains a menace to their livelihoods.

Alone among deeds to rival the jumping horses out in the country at The Festival are the tales of another warfare, the one down in the tumult of the betting ring. Across a span of 72 hours, the monoliths of the laying world will learn how their whole season has fared. It is a notion which occupies the biggest cat, Freddie Williams, as he travels south for the meeting.

"The build-up is an ongoing process," he says, "but it really starts to hit me when I come down from Scotland on the Monday night. I'm up there early on the Tuesday morning, looking across the course in anticipation of everything that's going to happen. But that's the trouble. You never know what is going to happen.

"The only thing you can be sure of is that it's a make or break week financially. If you have a good Festival, you have a good season. Full stop.

"It's a wee bit of a cliche, but before you actually get started it feels like there are butterflies flapping away down there."

The sweetest sound for Freddie Williams on the opening day is a different one. In his dreams he hears pattering on the windows. "Last year, with the top of the ground going, a lot of favourites and second favourites went in," he says. "There were some crushing blows over the three days. I'm anticipating getting my money back this year, which may be the worst thing in the world for me to believe. I might run into 15 favourites this year.

"The best results I've ever had at Cheltenham is when they've been up to their knees in muck, when their tongues are hanging out.

"There are nerves and other feelings because you know the big-hitters are going to be there. Taking more than £200,000 on a race at Cheltenham is easy. Once the prices go up though, it all disappears."

And once the chalk and numbers are on the boards the great anticipation is almost over. It is almost time for the roar.

Behind the scenes - preparing the course for the Festival: the sounds of drills, the scuffle of bins and the clip of a horse's newly shod hooves.

(above) *MLG*

(below) *TJ*

Facing: On course security is paramount.

Lunch for some, while others attend to the business of preparing the course.

(above left) *TJ*

(left) *TJ*

(above) *MLG*

Getting the best viewing spot means arriving early. While others would rather toast the success that is to come from their car boot.

(above) *MLG*

(above left) *TJ*

Left: Weeks of preparation may be over but for Clerk of the Course Simon Claisse (right) there's only time for a brief hello with trainer Nicky Henderson. *TJ*

L-R: Amateur Tom Greenway prepares to weigh out for the Kim Muir as Jim Culloty and Paul Flynn make their way to mount up for the National Hunt Chase.

Left: Jump Jockey turned radio commentator Luke Harvey waits for the cue with colleague Alice Plunkett in the parade ring. *TJ*

Below: Whether you have flash wheels or just four of them depends on how you work out the form.

(left) *TJ*

(right) *MLG*

Above: He may be the banker of the meeting but a little bit of lucky clover never went amiss. **MLG**

Right: It's all hats and tweeds for the jumping set. **TJ**

Left: Calm before the storm: Clerk of the Course Simon Claisse. *TJ*

Above: Moscow Flyer takes an early morning gallop. *EB*

Racecourse commentator Simon Holt enjoys a chat and a smoke before calling the action on one of jump racing's busiest days. *TJ*

No smoking here, but a roll in the sand is a perfect way to settle equine nerves. *MLG*

Lee McKenzie gets the focus on the turn for home. *TJ*

A friendly hello from trainer Jonjo O'Neill's wheels. *TJ*

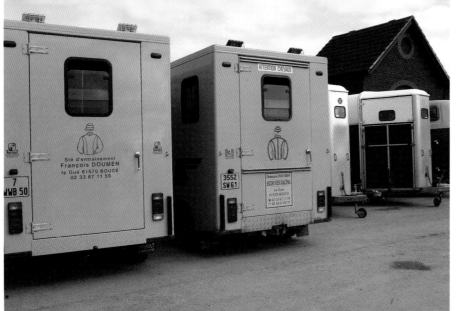

Facing: Stewards and racecourse officials make sure everything's in place before the first race.   *TJ*

Above: Triumphal arch from the JCB's.   *TJ*

Right: High roller.   *TJ*

Horses unboxed. Spit and polish. Valet sorts out the gear. **TJ**

Vets at the ready. A spick and span jockey's changing room.
A cheeky champion jockey dons his silks. **TJ**

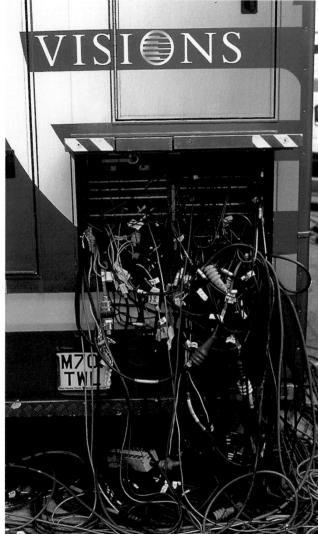

Facing top: Gentlemen of the press prepare their copy. **EB**

Facing bottom: Sir Clement Freud: no mobiles for a knight of the realm. **MLG**

Above: It takes miles and miles of cable for TV and radio to bring racing to the world outside.

(left & centre) **TJ**

(right) **MLG**

'Round and 'round they go as punters see what catches the eye. *TJ*

Chapter Four

Under Orders

Previous page: Charlie Swan parades the mighty Istabraq before the Smurfit Champion Hurdle.
TJ

Top & Right: Under starter's orders something goes 'face' - 5-2!
(top) *TJ*
(right) *MLG*

Facing: Discarded tickets litter the betting ring. *TJ*

Top Left: Foxchapel King with David Casey (left) and The Bunny Boiler, Paul Carberry presenting at the first fence in the National Hunt Handicap Chase. *TJ*

Bottom Left: Leaving the parade ring. *TJ*

Facing: Runners for the Fulke Walwyn Kim Muir Challenge Cup prepare for the race ahead. *TJ*

Top Right: Forgive & Forget leads runners to the start of the snowy 1987 Tote Gold Cup. *TJ*

Top Left: Final thoughts before the start. *TJ*

Bottom: All lined up and ready to go in the 2003 Tote Gold Cup. *TJ*

Right: The start – the crucial but often underplayed part of the race. *TJ*

Above: No sir, no sir! *TJ*

A few strides into history… the 2003 Tote Gold Cup. *TJ*

Facing: Over the last in the Fulke Walwyn Kim Muir. *TJ*

Chapter Five

Off and Running

All or nothing: the ups and downs of a champion jockey.

Top: Tony McCoy finishes a close second on Well Chief in the JCB Triumph Hurdle and (right) faces a long walk back after a fall on Le Roi Miguel. *TJ*

Left: Down the hill in the 1993 Coral Cup. **TJ**

Above: First circuit in the 2003 Pertemps Final Hurdle. **TJ**

Above: Up the straight for the first time in the 2003 Pertemps Final Hurdle. *TJ*

Right/Top: Four abreast in the 2000 Royal & SunAlliance Chase. *TJ*

Right/Middle: Kicking the birch in the 2000 Grand Annual Chase. *TJ*

Right/Bottom: Off at last in the snow in 1987. *TJ*

Left: First circuit in the 2003 Gold Cup: (L-R) Behrajan, Modulor, Colonel Braxton and See More Business. *TJ*

Below: Jockeying for position as the field sweeps past the packed grandstands. *TJ*

Below Left: His finest hour: the late Kieran Kelly drives home Hardy Eustace to win the 2003 Royal & SunAlliance Novices Hurdle. He died tragically that summer after a fall at Kilbeggan. *TJ*

The Spirit of Cheltenham 73

Double handfuls: Liam Cooper on Keen Leader and Barry Geraghty on Iris's Gift (right) look to be going smoothly enough. **TJ**

Above: A study in concentration - the 2003 William Hill National Hunt Steeplechase. **TJ**

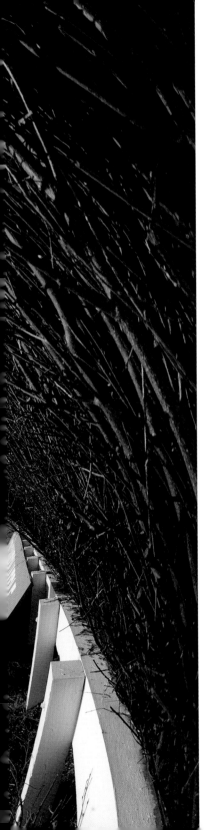

Left: Over the last in the 2003 William Hill National Hunt Steeplechase: (L-R) Haut Cercy, Youlneverwalkalone, Ad Hoc. *TJ*

Above: Moorlands Again and Joe Tizzard leads the field in the 133rd year of the National Hunt Steeplechase Challenge Cup. *TJ*

Following Pages: Anatomy of a fall. Tony McCoy hits the deck aboard Le Roi Miguel in the 2003 Irish Independent Arkle Chase. Both horse and jockey escaped unscathed. It was one of three falls the champion jockey took in a forgettable 2003 Festival week. *TJ*

Up and Running
By Tom O'Ryan (of the Racing Post)

The barked instruction from the starter's rostrum is clear, concise and cuts like a blade through the tension-filled atmosphere. "Make a line, jockeys!" Four words that forewarn and forearm. It's the moment you know there's no turning back. No hiding place. No escape from living out your dream.

The talking's over. Now it's time for action. Time to do the deed. Time to make a name for yourself. Everyone's thinking the same.

All around you, rival jockeys on proud and prancing horses are joshing and jostling, jousting for positions, squeezing, swearing and maybe even sweating. Just ahead is a single, white elastic tape. The dreaded scenario is losing ground, getting left behind. Seeing your mission aborted.

"Miss the break at Cheltenham," says Tote Gold Cup-winning rider Andrew Thornton, "and you might as well turn round and go home."

Concentration is the key. "C'mon, jockeys!" is the last thing you hear from the overhead rostrum as the tape pings away and the modern-day Charge of the Light Brigade begins. From then on, it's everyone for themselves.

Whether it's two miles, or three, fences or hurdles, it's all about finding the rhythm. Seeing the stride. Staying out of trouble. Speed and agility are your best weapons.

"Your horse has got to travel well," stresses Mick Fitzgerald, rider of 11 Festival winners. "Go down the inner on a horse, who is a bit one-paced, a bit slow to respond, and you'll get absolutely hammered. Gaps are there for only a split-second. To take them, you've got to have plenty of 'boot', because when you see them opening, you can be sure that the two jockeys nearest to you will see them as well and will be going for the same 'hole.' And," adds the bold Fitzy with a knowing smile, "three-into-one doesn't go!"

Friends in the weighing-room become foes on the course. There's too much at stake to be 'nice.' Request a favour in the heat of battle? The chances are that the jockey crowding you on the approach to an obstacle, will suddenly become deaf as a post as you scream for an inch of daylight.

"If you're pushing along on a horse, struggling to hold its place, you're going to get squeezed out, knocked back or pushed wide," says Jim Culloty. Not though, if you're on a superstar like Best Mate.

Culloty had no had no such problems last year, or the year before, on the dual Tote Gold Cup winner. "The crucial thing," he points out, "is having plenty of horse under you."

Upright trouble-spots along the way are plentiful. "The second open-ditch on the final circuit of the Tote Gold Cup course is probably the trickiest on the track," says Thornton, as he targets the potential danger, five fences from the finish. "The race is starting in earnest. Horses are just starting to come off the bridle. The worry is that they'll stand-off too far and leave their hind legs behind."

Courage and commitment are vital. "You've got to be definite, very definite there," stresses Fitzgerald. "If you go in on a long stride, you've got to capitalize and make sure you get there. A good jump can gain you lengths. And set you up for the next."

Four fences from the finish in the Tote Gold Cup is, according to Fitzgerald, "make-or-break time." Angled, just before a sharp left-hand bend, it possesses hidden dangers. "Make a move at the wrong time, and you'll put your horse off his stride," explains Fitzgerald. "You must have them balanced."

You must also hold your nerve. The finish is in sight. Andrew Thornton's first-ever ride at The Festival was a winning one. Aboard the staying chaser Maamur back in 1996. "Turning into the home straight, I'll always remember saying to myself – over and over again – 'think you're at Plumpton,'" he recalls. "Cheltenham is Cheltenham, but you just can't afford to lose your head and get carried away."

Even worse is being carried away in an ambulance. Vinny Keane may have been spared that gut-wrenching experience at each of the last two Festival jamborees. But what he wasn't spared, both times, was hitting the turf two from home in the Queen Mother Champion Chase when challenging for the lead on the bold-jumping Latalomne.

Is it any wonder that he beat the ground with his whip in sheer frustration? Any surprise that the agony of his late departure - being cheated out of his chance of glory, not once, but twice - brought tears to his eyes? Hardly.

Winning a Queen Mother Champion Chase, a Smurfit Champion Hurdle, a Tote Gold Cup – any race at the Festival – is the ultimate thrill, the achievement that sets you apart.

It's all about crossing that finishing line first. Savouring the moment as you parade back past the packed stands to the unsaddling enclosure. Arm raised in triumph, ears filled with 60,000 cheers and head and heart filled with elation and excitement, undiluted joy and wholesome relief that your mission has ended in triumph.

"It's the most brilliant feeling," says Mick Fitzgerald, echoing the thoughts of every jockey, who has ever ridden this world-famous circuit. "There's nothing better than winning at Cheltenham…"

A last hurdle blunder by Royal Emperor gives Inching Closer and Barry Geraghty (left) a chance in the 2003 Pertemps Final Handicap Hurdle. *TJ*

Kieran Kelly and Hardy Eustace beat
Tony Dobbin and Coolnagorna in the
2003 Royal & SunAlliance Novices
Hurdle. *TJ*

Barry Geraghty and Spectroscope (right)
edges out Tony McCoy and Well Chief in
the 2003 JCB Triumph Hurdle. *TJ*

Top Left: Mick Fitzgerald on Xenophon gets up to beat David Casey on Samon in the Coral Cup. *TJ*

Top Right: Barry Geraghty and Youlneverwalkalone (left) stalk Richard Johnson and Haut Cercy in the William Hill National Hunt Chase. *TJ*

Bottom Right: A foot perfect Rooster Booster and Richard Johnson take the Smurfit Champion Hurdle. *TJ*

Facing: Larry McGrath and Ibis Rochelais, second in the Fulke Walwyn Kim Muir. *TJ*

Barry Geraghty drives Inching Closer (left) to beat Dominic Elsworth and Royal Emperor by a short head in the 2003 Pertemps Final Handicap Hurdle. *TJ*

Modern technology separates winners and losers. *TJ*

Facing: Ruby Walsh punches the air after winning the 2003 Irish Independent Arkle on Azertyuiop. *TJ*

Chapter Six

Winning & Losing

Back in Front and Norman Williamson land the gamble in the 2003 Festival opener. *TJ*

Unseated in the 1999 Fulke Walwyn Kim Muir. *TJ*

Above: Returning. **TJ**

Right: Kingscliff, impressive winner of the 2003 Christie's Foxhunter Chase. **TJ**

The screens go up: the worst sight of all on any racecourse. *TJ*

Above: Azertyuiop wins the Irish Independent Arkle. *TJ*

Right: Mr DW Cullen returns with saddle but otherwise empty handed. *TJ*

Jim Culloty salutes an emphatic victory for Best Mate's second Tote Gold Cup. **TJ**

Above: Tony McCoy reflects on a fall. *TJ*

Right: Barry Geraghty is ecstatic after winning the Queen Mother
Champion Chase on Jessica Harrington's Moscow Flyer. *TJ*

Unsaddling after a fall. *TJ*

One of the joys of Cheltenham: win, lose or draw you
can get close to the horses after the race. *TJ*

Azertyuiop wins the Irish Independent Arkle in impressive style. *TJ*

Stormin' home: Norman Williamson drives Back in Front home to win the 2003 Gerrard Supreme Novices' Hurdle by ten lengths for trainer Eddy O'Grady and land a massive Irish gamble. **TJ**

Left: A beaming Polly Gundry returns after finishing second in the Christie's Foxhunters on Bright Approach. Meanwhile (above) in any race it's coming home safe and sound that really counts. *TJ*

Left: Richard Johnson drives home Rooster Booster in the Smurfit Champion Hurdle. **TJ**

Top: Connections celebrate the win. **TJ**

L-R: Herself an accomplished horsewoman, Princess Anne congratulates Moscow Flyer's owners
Mr & Mrs Brian Kearney on winning the Queen Mother Champion Chase. ***TJ***

Heroes All *by Jon Freeman*

Cheltenham's come and Cheltenham's go and every year something happens that will stick in the mind forever. But just as the pop music was much better in dad's day, so it was at The Festival; you lot may have Radiohead and Rooster Booster, but when I was a lad we had Bula and The Beatles. No contest!

The truth is probably that we always remember best and admire most what we heard or saw when we were most impressionable, although I still find it hard to concede that there has been anything more thrilling than the Tote Gold Cup victories of Dawn Run and Desert Orchid or more exhilarating than the subsequent celebrations.

Every winner, especially an Irish winner, at The Festival is greeted by a thunderous roar, it has become a sort of tradition, but when Dawn Run and Desert Orchid returned after their heroics, it was something else again. 50,000 people cheering and shouting as loudly as they could, some of them hugging complete strangers, others with tears in their eyes as the emotion of it all got the better of them.

Both the Irish mare and Dessie were sent off as favourites, but this was about more than just money. The other day I had a good look of that famous photograph of Jonjo O'Neill punching the air in triumph as he brought Dawn Run back through a throng of deliriously excited fans to the winner's enclosure after the mare had become the first ever to win both the Smurfit Champion Hurdle and Tote Gold Cup. There, just off to the right, was Jimmy FitzGerald beaming and clapping them home, his sense of the moment overriding the disappointment he must have felt as Dawn Run overtook his own Forgive'n Forget in that dramatic dash to the line.

Three years later, in 1989, everybody's favourite white horse, Desert Orchid, won his Tote Gold Cup in much the same fashion as Dawn Run, rallying going to the last fence to regain the advantage over Yahoo, who had looked sure to spring an unpopular surprise turning into the home straight.

I watched the race with a friend who had backed Yahoo ante-post at 66-1. "Go on Yahoo," he screamed, not unreasonably in the circumstances, as his long-shot went past Desert Orchid in a seemingly decisive move. Then silence for a few seconds as Dessie responded to the urgings of the other 49,999 at Prestbury. And then, believe it or not, another shout of encouragement - "Go on Dessie," - as he kissed his big win goodbye, bowed to the inevitable outcome and joined in with the rest of us in cheering home a wonderful champion.

Racing is a sport as well as a betting medium and nowhere do the two sides live together more cordially than at Cheltenham. Like every other Festival regular, I have had my ups and downs as a punter over the years, but as my friend said after that costly near miss: "It's a pleasure to do your money at this meeting."

One thing punters should be clear about is that the best horses do not always win the best races at Cheltenham. The demands of the track are quite different to say, Kempton, which is why such as Desert Orchid, Wayward Lad (runner-up to Dawn Run) and later One Man found winning the Tote Gold Cup so much harder than winning the King George Chase, which they did nine times between them.

Those three were such good jumpers that they were never inconvenienced unduly by Cheltenham's stiff fences, but they still couldn't quite manage to quite run up to the form they displayed elsewhere on flatter circuits.

By the time Desert Orchid had won his Tote Gold Cup, he had become the most popular horse in the country, but though it was one of his most memorable performances, it was by no means his best and he was unable to repeat the feat in 1990 when regarded by some as a 'certainty.'

Wayward Lad was a champion wherever he ran, except at Cheltenham, where the final hill would catch him out. One Man, like Dessie a bold-jumping grey and a great favourite with the public, could win over three

miles and more at Kempton and Newbury, but twice his legs turned to jelly in the stamina-sapping home straight at Cheltenham and in the end he had to settle for the Festival's two-mile crown.

Some of the best hurdlers have been found out by the Cheltenham hill, too. Sea Pigeon came to challenge Monksfield at the last on the bridle in both 1978 and 1979, but when push came to shove he couldn't manage the Irish raider's strength in the finish.

He gained his revenge on Monksfield the following season (and won it again in 1981), but probably only because the Smurfit Champion Hurdle course was made less demanding (it used to include a run up the hill on the first circuit as well).

The Smurfit Champion Hurdle has been won more than once by several famous names since the war: National Spirit (twice), Hatton's Grace (three times), Sir Ken (three), Persian War (three), Bula (two), Comedy Of Errors (two), Night Nurse (two), Monksfield (two), Sea Pigeon (two), See You Then (three) and most recently Istabraq (three and it may well have been four if the 2001 Festival hadn't been lost to the foot and mouth epidemic).

In contrast the Tote Gold Cup has rarely been won by a horse more than once since the most famous chaser of them all, Arkle, won it three times in the mid sixties. Several have gone close, but only L'Escargot managed to win back-to-back Gold Cups (1970 and 1971) before Best Mate proved it could still be done in 2002 and last spring.

A third win for Best Mate in March would just about bring Prestbury's smart new house down and even the grumpiest among us will join in with the noisy acclaim and be happy to concede that Henrietta Knight's chaser is one of the all-time greats. Shame about the pop music, though.

Barry Geraghty brings home Moscow Flyer in fine style to win the Queen Mother Champion Chase and gets a rousing reception from the crowd. *TJ*

Above & Left: Trainer Nicky Henderson celebrates at the 2001 Festival. *TJ*

Facing: Paul Nicholls greets his young star Azertyuiop. *TJ*

Richard Johnson returns victorious on Rooster Booster, one of his four winners at the 2003 Festival. *TJ*

With five winners, Barry Geraghty took the riding honours at the 2003 Festival. *TJ*

Facing: Amateur Seamus McHugh checks the scales after winning the Fulke Walwyn Kim Muir Handicap Chase on Royal Predica for Martin Pipe. *TJ*

Right: Racecourse Chairman Lord Vestey introduces the winners in the parade ring. *TJ*

Left & Above: Hen party: A hug from hubby Terry, kisses from owner Jim Lewis and jockey Jim Culloty after emerging from her hiding place for Best Mate's second Tote Gold Cup win. **TJ**

Facing: Trophies from HM The Queen for trainer, owner and jockey. **TJ**

Above: Gallic flair: Trainer Francois Doumen congratulates son Thierry on winning the Bonusprint Stayers' Hurdle on Baracouda for owner JP McManus (right). ***TJ***

Chapter Seven

Great Moments

The people's hero: despite doubts about staying the trip, sheer guts brought Desert Orchid home to win the 1989 Tote Gold Cup for owner Richard Burridge and Janice Coyle. The grey also twice finished third. *TJ*

Andrew Thornton springs a surprise victory in the 1998 Tote Gold Cup aboard 25-1 shot Cool Dawn. *TJ*

Imperial Call under Conor O'Dwyer wins the 1996 Tote Gold Cup and returns to a rapturous welcome. *TJ*

Facing: Mark Pitman wins the 1991 Tote Gold Cup for his mother and trainer Jenny aboard Garrison Savannah. *TJ*

Top left: Bookie's benefit: 100-1 shocker Norton's Coin wins the 1990 Tote Gold Cup for Welsh Farmer Sirrell Griffiths. *TJ*

Top right: Vive la France: The Fellow under Adam Kondrat wins the 1994 Tote Gold Cup for Francois Doumen. *TJ*

Bottom right: Pearlyman, twice winner of the Queen Mother Champion Chase in 1987 and 1988. *TJ*

Bottom left: Spectacular jumper and athlete Remittance Man. *TJ*

The Thinker goes for gold in the 1987 Tote
Gold Cup from Cybrandian and Doorlatch. *TJ*

As game as they come: Viking Flagship twice came up trumps in the 1994 and 1995 editions of the Queen Mother Champion Chase. *TJ*

Tony McCoy steals the 1997 Smurfit Champion Hurdle with an all the way win aboard Make A Stand for Martin Pipe. *TJ*

Facing:

Top left: Celtic Shot takes the 1988 Smurfit Champion Hurdle from Classical Charm and Celtic Chief. *TJ*

Bottom left & right: See You Then's Smurfit Champion Hurdle victory at the snowy 1987 Festival. He won the race three years running from 1985-87. *TJ*

Millennium winner: Looks Like Trouble and Richard Johnson break
Irish hearts by beating Florida Pearl in the Tote Gold Cup. *TJ*

Ageless campaigner Edredon Bleu wins the 2000
Queen Mother Champion Chase for Tony McCoy
and the Henrietta Knight and Jim Lewis team. *TJ*

Top left: Dropped back in distance after disappointing in the Tote Gold Cup, One Man gains victory in the 1998 Queen Mother Champion Chase. *TJ*

Bottom left: So near, so far: Wayward Lad and Graham Bradley came second in the 1986 Tote Gold Cup. He was perhaps the best chaser never to win a Tote Gold Cup. *TJ*

Top right: Mr Mulligan and Tony McCoy team up to give Noel Chance a victory in the 1997 Tote Gold Cup. *TJ*

Bottom right: Evens favourite Carvill's Hill leads the first circuit of the 1992 Tote Gold Cup. *TJ*

Stars and stripes: American owned Flagship Uberalles takes the 2003 edition of the Queen Mother Champion Chase. *TJ*

Mick Fitzgerald and See More Business (left) catch long shot Go
Ballistic at the last and go on to victory in the 1999 Tote Gold Cup. *TJ*

Chapter Eight

The Spirit of Cheltenham

Facing: Top Left: Sir Peter O'Sullevan, the voice of racing. **TJ**

Bottom Left: Owner Lord Andrew Lloyd Webber. **MLG**

Right: Camera man needs a steady hand. **TJ**

Above left: Jockey Club PR Director John Maxse. **TJ**

Right: A Royal occasion: HM The Queen with Tony McCoy, Lord Vestey and former jumps trainer Michael Dickinson, famous for saddling the first five home in the 1983 Tote Gold Cup. **TJ**

Above: Everyone needs a hat. **MLG**

Right: Owner Sir Robert Ogden. **TJ**

All eyes are on Zara Phillips, Hon President of Cheltenham's Club 16-24. *TJ*

Stands, seats and crowds in the Guinness enclosure. *TJ*

A quiet moment before the day gets going. *MLG*

Above: Preparing for the off. *MLG*

Left: Trainer Francois & Elizabeth Doumen walk the course before Baracouda wins the Bonusprint Stayers' Hurdle. *TJ*

Above: Straight from the horse's mouth: racing personality and pundit John McCririck. **MLG**

Right: Bets and beer – punters prepare to take on the old enemy. **MLG**

Readies for the off.
(above) *TJ*
(right) *MLG*

On the rails. *TJ*

When the chips are down
many turn to the booze. *MLG*

Above & Right: Keeping body and soul together. **TJ**

Right: Norman Williamson sits this one out. **TJ**

Facing:

Left: Writer Julian Muscat (left) chats with Michael Dickinson and his mother Monica. **TJ**

Top: A sporty Paul Nicholls. **TJ**

Bottom: Martin Pipe on the phone, what else? **TJ**

Coats and hats galore… *TJ*

And something for the ladies… **TJ**

And for kids of all ages.

(top) *TJ*

(right) *MLG*

There's still work to be done, whether it's shovelling coal or replacing divots. **TJ**

One furlong from
the Holy Grail. *TJ*

Tote Chairman Peter Jones (left) raises a laugh from HM The Queen and Jim Culloty. *TJ*

Gone but not forgotten: The Queen unveils
the bust of Cheltenham's greatest fan,
HM The Queen Mother 1900-2002. **TJ**

The Spirit of Cheltenham *by Alastair Down*

Ritual gatherings have a mystique all their own. There is something both uncanny and awesome about the great animal migrations, be they caribou or wildesbeest, elvers or whales. Every year some primeval urge moves all of them in vast numbers to undertake perilous journeys to a place which some unfathomable part of their psyche compels them to attend.

In late spring, as the trees are breaking into leaf, the same family of swallows arrive on the telephone wires outside my house just half an hour across the top of the Cotswolds from Cheltenham racecourse. They have flown over five thousand miles from Africa to return to the same nondescript garage where they raised their last brood of young. Six months later they take wing again on the treacherous trek back to the Dark Continent, but as I watch them and their young preparing for this most astonishing of journeys I know they will return to my neck of Gloucestershire once more. And of course for those passionate about Cheltenham some of the rituals are just as infallibly observed. Come March from all corners of the Islands as wide a cross section of humanity as it is possible to imagine make their way to Cheltenham for the Festival. It is never a spur of the moment journey, those three days aren't blocked off in the calendar weeks or even months before, they are blocked off for life.

In pubs, hotels and B and B's the same groups of friends gather for the great event, have a drink or a meal with fellow enthusiasts they run into just once a year and get their teeth into the things that really matter -what's going to be winning over the three most exciting days in sport. For connoisseurs of atmosphere there is nothing to match The Cheltenham Festival. Its addictive appeal has many strands - the matchless seating in the lee of Cleeve Hill, the severity of the questions asked, the intense rivalry between Britain and Ireland that unites more than it divides and the sheer sense of celebration.

And it is every type person. The great and good rubbing shoulders with the decidedly dodgy and all part of a democracy of the dedicated who know full well that each day will produce the very stuff of racing legend, that in front of their eyes fresh legends will be forged.

There is always the knowledge that, in so many ways, the entire racing year boils down to these few hours. That all the strands of racing's web lead to this single time and place when the questions of months receive the answers of minutes.

The crowd knows that every horse that comes up that hill in front will have passed through the fire. There are no easy victories at Cheltenham, the course is an unyielding test and the level of competition flares with astonishing intensity. Those who believe that we cold folk of Northern Europe can not match our Latin brethren in terms of public displays of emotion should watch a festival winner come down the horsewalk in front of the stands as they erupt in acclaim. And to see the reception horse and rider recieves as they make their way into the winner's enclosure is to witness an amazing display of pure feeling - an almost toxic cocktail of joy, relief, gratitude and admiration.

This is sport in the raw, dangerous yet beautiful, compelling and almost unwatcheable at the same time.

And somehow, out of the packed bars, the clogged walkways, the sardine tins of the stands or betting ring and the steaming horses comes some indefinable piece of chemistry that is utterly compulsive. For most of the Festival crowd it is simply a question of having to be there, of answering some call that is beyond resisting - they would no more consider being anywhere else on that particular afternoon than fly to the moon. At its very best, sport can be a tremendously enriching force. And Cheltenham manages that rare feat with wonderful regularity. The spirit of Cheltenham is potent indeed and those who drink deep of know that nothing else tastes quite the same.

Sheer Nectar *MLG*

Very smart. *TJ*

Not so smart. *MLG*

Life is a merry go round, and no more so than at the races. *TJ*

Above: Goodnight Cheltenham. ***EB***

Facing: Safely home. ***TJ***

Chapter Nine

At the end of the day

Homeward bound. *MLG*

Full steam ahead! *TJ*

Facing: A study in racing legends -
Dawn Run and Jonjo O'Neill. *TJ*

Right: Returning to the racecourse stables. *TJ*

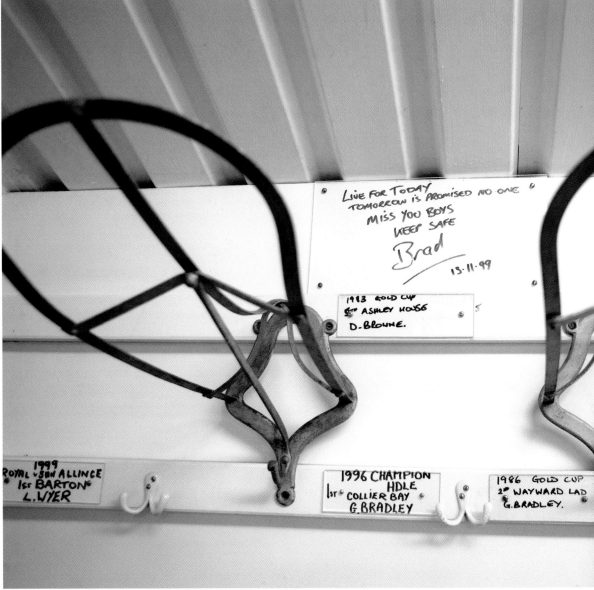

Suits you. *MLG*

Mementoes and Memories. Names from the past to set the mind racing. *TJ*

Stylish. **MLG**   Less stylish. **EB**

How was your day? **MLG**

Painted ponies. **MLG**

Hall of Fame. *TJ*

Left: Remembering Dessie and others

Facing: Remembering Kieran Kelly.

Left: (Top) Willie Mullins with Alexander Banquet (left) and Florida Pearl. ***CN***

Bottom: Florida Pearl with Tracy Gilmour and Max. ***CN***

Boxed and roughed off. *TJ*

Tomorrow's another day. **_TJ_**